How Microchips Work

The Science Behind the Billion-Transistor Revolution

Owen Delaney

Copyright

Disclaimer

This book is intended for informational and educational purposes only. While every effort has been made to ensure the accuracy and reliability of the content, the author and publisher make no guarantees regarding its completeness, correctness, or applicability to any specific situation. The field of semiconductor technology is constantly evolving, and new advancements, regulations, and industry standards may emerge that are not covered in this book.

The author and publisher disclaim any liability for any errors, omissions, or consequences resulting from the use of the information contained herein. Readers are encouraged to conduct their own research and consult with professionals or experts in the field before making decisions related to semiconductor technology, manufacturing, or business strategies.

Additionally, this book does not provide professional, legal, financial, or technical advice. Any references to specific companies, technologies, or historical events are for illustrative purposes only and do not imply endorsement or affiliation. Any resemblance to real-life individuals or proprietary information is purely coincidental.

Table Of Contents

Introduction

Imagine holding the device you're reading this on right now—a smartphone, tablet, or computer. Now, pause for a moment and consider the complexity of that seemingly simple device. How does it work? What drives the instant responses when you tap a screen, swipe, or speak a command? What powers the apps that keep you connected to the world? The answer, in a nutshell, lies in something so small, yet so mighty: microchips.

In every facet of our modern lives—whether it's the phone in your pocket, the car you drive, the medical equipment that saves lives, or the appliances in your home—microchips are at work, silently enabling the technology we often take for granted. These tiny devices are the foundation upon which our entire digital world is built. They are the unseen architects of the devices we rely on and the unsung heroes of the digital age.

But despite their immense importance, how often do we stop to consider what goes into making these technological marvels? How do they work? How did we go from the early days of rudimentary electrical circuits to the intricate billion-transistor chips that power today's most sophisticated devices? The journey of microchips from mere sand to the marvels of silicon is nothing short of awe-inspiring.

Microchips are not just the building blocks of individual gadgets; they are the heart and soul of the entire digital infrastructure that powers our modern world. At the core of every device, from the simplest calculator to the most advanced supercomputer, lies a microchip. These chips carry out the calculations, store the data, and execute the instructions that make our devices functional. They are at the center of everything we do—from sending emails to exploring the vastness of space.

But how did we arrive at this point? To understand the revolutionary impact microchips have had, we must first grasp the complexity and precision involved in their creation. What might seem like a simple component is actually the result of millions of hours of research, design, and development—an achievement of human ingenuity that has transformed the world as we know it.

We live in an era where microchips are the driving force behind all technological advancements. They enable artificial intelligence, quantum computing, the Internet of Things (IoT), self-driving cars, and much more. Every advancement in computing power, data storage, and processing speed has been made possible by the progress in microchip technology. But this wasn't always the case. In fact, the very concept of a microchip was born out of necessity and ingenuity—a desire to make computers smaller, faster, and more efficient, so they could be more accessible and practical for the masses.

The humble beginnings of microchips trace back to the early 20th century, when engineers and scientists first sought to improve the performance of electronic circuits. As technology progressed, the idea of creating a single chip that could house thousands, then millions, and eventually billions of transistors began to take shape. The challenges faced along the way were immense, but the rewards—instant computing power at a fraction of the size and cost of previous technologies—have been game-changing.

We live in a time when technology is evolving at an unprecedented pace. And at the core of that evolution is the microchip. In fact, microchips are so pervasive that they often go unnoticed. Yet, without them, the world we live in today would cease to function in the way we know it.

Have you ever wondered how it is possible for a single chip to power your smartphone, a device that connects you to the internet, runs multiple apps simultaneously, and processes high-definition video—all at lightning speed? How is it that these small chips can handle enormous amounts of data and make decisions in real-time? The answer lies in the design and technology behind them, and understanding this process is crucial for anyone wishing to grasp the future of technology.

This book is an invitation to delve into the fascinating world of microchip technology, where silicon, transistors, and billions of electrical impulses come together to shape the future. It's an exploration of how these seemingly invisible devices work, how they're created, and why they are so central to our technological advancement. Whether you're a tech enthusiast, a student, or someone simply curious about the wonders of modern life, understanding microchips is key to appreciating the digital landscape that surrounds us.

Microchips have transformed nearly every industry, from healthcare and telecommunications to entertainment and transportation. They allow us to perform tasks faster, more efficiently, and with greater accuracy than ever before. In fact, the success of almost all modern innovations, from space exploration to artificial intelligence, hinges on the advances in microchip technology. As we continue to push the boundaries of what's possible, the role of microchips will only grow in importance. Understanding how they work and why they are so essential will give you a deeper appreciation for the incredible advancements in technology that are shaping the world.

The Journey from Sand to Silicon: An Awe-Inspiring Process

At the heart of every microchip lies silicon, a naturally abundant element found in sand. The journey from sand to silicon is one of the most fascinating transformations in the world of technology. It's a story of how a raw material—commonly found on the shores of beaches or in the depths of deserts—undergoes a meticulous and highly sophisticated process to become the backbone of the most powerful computing systems on Earth.

Silicon, in its raw form, is far from the high-tech material that powers our microchips. It starts as a dull, grayish substance found in quartz rocks or sand. But through a remarkable series of chemical and physical processes, silicon is purified, refined, and transformed into the sleek, shiny wafers used in semiconductor manufacturing. These wafers, typically less than half a millimeter thick, serve as the foundation upon which billions of transistors will be built, creating the intricate circuits that power our devices.

But how does this transformation occur? The process begins in a semiconductor fabrication plant, where silicon wafers are meticulously crafted using highly precise equipment. It takes specialized machinery and advanced techniques to purify the silicon, remove impurities, and shape it into a usable form. Once the raw silicon is ready, it is sliced into thin wafers, polished to a mirror-like finish, and treated with a variety of chemical and physical processes to prepare it for the next stage of production.

Next comes the intricate process of building the transistors and creating the complex circuits that will eventually form the heart of the microchip. Each transistor, a tiny electronic switch that controls the flow of electricity, must be precisely positioned on the silicon wafer. The process involves multiple layers of materials being deposited, etched, and treated, all while maintaining absolute precision to ensure that each transistor functions as intended.

As these layers of materials are built upon the wafer, the transistors become smaller and more densely packed, allowing more functionality to be crammed into an ever-smaller space. The process is highly complex, requiring millions of dollars in equipment and facilities, as well as an incredible amount of expertise and precision. And, throughout this entire process, even the smallest mistake can result in a defective chip, rendering it useless.

Finally, once the microchip is complete, it undergoes rigorous testing to ensure it meets the exacting standards required for commercial use. The chip is tested for performance, reliability, and heat resistance, as well as for its ability to handle the vast amounts of data that will pass through it once it's deployed in the real world. Once it passes these tests, the chip is packaged and prepared for sale.

This entire journey—from raw sand to powerful microchip—takes place in a highly controlled, clean environment, known as a cleanroom, where even the tiniest speck of dust can ruin the delicate process. Each step of the journey is a masterpiece of engineering and precision, and it's this intricate process that makes modern microchips so incredibly powerful.

As you continue through this book, you'll discover the science, the process, and the innovations that go into creating the microchips that power our world. You'll uncover the hidden magic behind the smallest of technologies, and perhaps for the first time, you'll begin to understand how microchips—these tiny, almost invisible devices—are actually the giant forces driving our digital revolution. Welcome to the extraordinary world of microchips, where science meets innovation, and the future of technology is being built, layer by layer, one nanometer at a time.

The Promise of This Book

As you venture further into the pages of this book, you'll unlock a treasure trove of knowledge that unravels the science, process, and real-world significance of microchips. This is not just a technical manual or a dry analysis—this is a journey into the heart of the technology that shapes our modern world, told in a way that's engaging, easy to understand, and filled with fascinating insights.

First and foremost, this book will give you a deep dive into the fascinating science behind microchips. We'll explore how these tiny devices, made from silicon—the same material found in sand—are transformed into the backbone of nearly every piece of technology we use. You'll learn about the intricate process of creating microchips, from the basic principles of semiconductor physics to the cutting-edge technologies used to create billions of transistors on a single chip. This is not just about understanding circuits and wires, but how these components interact at the atomic level to make our devices work.

You'll also gain insight into how transistors, the building blocks of microchips, function as tiny electronic switches that control the flow of electricity. We'll explain how these switches operate in unison to process information, execute commands, and handle complex calculations that power everything from your phone to the cloud. By the end of this book, you'll not only understand what microchips do but how they do it in the most efficient and powerful way imaginable.

One of the most awe-inspiring aspects of microchips is the manufacturing process. Microchip fabrication is an art, a science, and a feat of engineering that requires precision on an atomic scale. The process is so intricate that even the slightest misstep can render a chip useless. In this book, we'll walk you through every stage of microchip production—from the creation of silicon wafers, to the step-by-step layering of transistors and interconnects, to the rigorous testing and packaging that ensures each chip functions as intended.

You'll learn about the cleanroom environments where these chips are made, where the tiniest speck of dust can ruin an entire batch. You'll also discover how advanced machinery and tools, which cost millions of dollars, are used to etch the microscopic circuits that allow each chip to carry out its tasks. This part of the book will provide you with a behind-the-scenes look at the incredible complexity and precision involved in crafting the microchips that power the devices we use every day.

While the science and process are fascinating in their own right, what truly sets this book apart is its focus on the real-world significance of microchips. After all, what good is understanding the theory and process behind microchips if you don't understand how they impact your life?

In this book, you will explore how microchips are the driving force behind nearly every technological advancement in the modern world. We'll show you how these chips power everything from the smartphones in your pocket to the artificial intelligence systems that are reshaping industries. Microchips are the silent enablers of innovations in fields as diverse as healthcare, transportation, entertainment, communications, and even space exploration. They make it possible for us to perform everyday tasks with speed, efficiency, and accuracy.

You'll also learn about the future of microchip technology. With the advent of smaller, faster, and more powerful chips, we're on the brink of a technological revolution that could change the way we live, work, and interact with the world. From the growth of the Internet of Things (IoT) to breakthroughs in quantum computing, microchips will be at the center of it all. This book will give you a glimpse into what's coming next, and how the tiny chips of today are paving the way for the world of tomorrow.

By the time you finish this book, you will have gained a comprehensive understanding of microchips, their creation, and their importance in our modern world. You'll have an appreciation for the incredible complexity that goes into making these seemingly simple devices. And most importantly, you'll understand just how pivotal microchips are to the technology that powers our lives.

But this is not just a book for engineers or tech enthusiasts. Whether you're someone who's simply curious about the devices you use every day, a student eager to learn more about the technologies shaping the future, or a professional in the tech industry, you'll find valuable insights in these pages. This book is designed to be accessible, engaging, and informative—no matter your background or level of expertise.

So, get ready to embark on an enlightening journey into the world of microchips. You'll discover the science, the process, and the real-world significance of these tiny but powerful components that are, quite literally, changing the world. With every page, you'll gain a deeper understanding of the technology that drives the future, and you might just find yourself looking at the world around you in a whole new light.

Chapter 1

From Sand to Silicon – The Birth of Microchips

The foundation of every electronic device, from the smartphone in your pocket to the car you drive, begins with something simple—sand. But what seems like an ordinary, easily overlooked material actually holds the secret to the most advanced technology that powers the modern world. This chapter takes you on an extraordinary journey from sand to silicon, revealing how this unassuming element is transformed into the backbone of all microchips—the tiny yet powerful components that drive the digital age.

In today's interconnected world, microchips are so deeply embedded in our daily lives that it's almost impossible to imagine a time without them. Yet, these marvels of engineering didn't just appear overnight. They are the result of decades of research, innovation, and mastery over materials that initially seem unremarkable.

As you follow this journey from sand to silicon, you will learn why silicon is uniquely suited to the role of creating microchips. You'll understand how this naturally abundant material is refined, shaped, and turned into a precision instrument capable of housing billions of transistors. From the initial discovery of silicon's potential to its transformation in cleanrooms that resemble spaceships more than factories, every step in the process is a testament to human ingenuity and the relentless drive to build something from nothing.

You will also uncover the high-tech environment in which microchips are made. In state-of-the-art fabrication plants, a highly controlled, dust-free environment is crucial for the success of microchip manufacturing. These plants, often spanning the size of multiple football fields, are filled with machinery costing millions of dollars, working tirelessly to create microchips that will power the devices shaping our world. Here, every detail matters, and one mistake can render an entire batch of microchips useless.

Finally, we will take a closer look at the staggering cost and investment required to produce microchips. A single silicon wafer, which might start out costing only a few hundred dollars, can become a product worth up to $100,000 once it's populated with the intricate circuitry that makes up a microchip. This chapter will provide insight into the financial stakes of microchip manufacturing and reveal how every single dollar spent contributes to the transformation of a raw material into one of the most valuable components in technology.

By the end of this chapter, you'll have a comprehensive understanding of how something as simple as sand can be transformed into the most powerful, life-changing technology humanity has ever known.

The Origins of Silicon

Silicon's journey to becoming the material at the heart of microchips begins in the earth, in the form of sand. Silica, a compound made of silicon and oxygen, is the second most abundant mineral on Earth. But how did we go from sand—something we walk on every day—to a material that powers our smartphones, computers, and even spacecraft?

Silicon, in its raw form, is a metalloid, meaning it has properties of both metals and non-metals. It is not naturally in a pure state but is usually found in compounds like silicon dioxide, which is the main component of sand. To harness the full potential of silicon, it must first be extracted and refined into pure silicon. This transformation is far from simple. The raw material undergoes several stages of refinement, including heating in furnaces to remove impurities. The resulting pure silicon is then melted down and carefully cooled into cylindrical forms called ingots. These ingots are sliced into thin wafers, which will serve as the foundation for microchips.

What makes silicon ideal for this purpose is its unique properties. As a semiconductor, silicon has the ability to both conduct and insulate electricity, depending on its state. When carefully manipulated, silicon can be used to create transistors—tiny switches that can control the flow of electrical current. This is the core function of microchips, where billions of these transistors work together to perform complex tasks in devices we use every day.

In addition to its electrical properties, silicon is abundant, non-toxic, and relatively easy to process. These advantages made it the perfect candidate for use in the rapidly growing field of electronics. Once silicon's potential was recognized, scientists and engineers set to work creating processes to refine it into the high-quality material needed for microchips. Through these efforts, silicon became not just a part of the natural world, but an indispensable element of the digital revolution.

The Journey of Sand Being Transformed into Pure Silicon Wafers

The journey from sand to silicon wafer is nothing short of a modern-day alchemical process. First, the sand is heated to incredibly high temperatures in furnaces, often reaching up to 2,000°C (3,632°F), to separate the silicon from the oxygen it is bound to in the form of silicon dioxide. This is done by adding carbon, which bonds with the oxygen, leaving behind pure silicon. The silicon is then cooled into large, cylindrical shapes known as ingots.

These ingots are sliced into thin wafers, each just a few millimeters thick. These wafers serve as the foundational surface on which the microchip will be built. At this stage, the silicon is still a far cry from the powerful microchips that will one day be used in everything from laptops to medical devices. It must undergo a series of intricate and precise processes before it can be considered ready for use in microchip fabrication.

These processes, which take place in semiconductor fabrication plants, are far from straightforward. Each step must be done with immense precision. Even the smallest speck of dust or the tiniest error in temperature can ruin an entire batch of silicon wafers. The wafers must be cleaned and prepared before they can move on to the next stages of the microchip manufacturing process, which involves adding layers of materials, etching circuits, and assembling the tiny transistors that make up the microchip.

The transformation of raw silicon into usable microchips is a feat of modern engineering, involving countless hours of work and a level of precision that borders on the impossible. What began as sand is now ready to be turned into one of the most advanced and essential components of modern technology.

The Cleanroom Environment

Inside a semiconductor fabrication plant, the production of microchips takes place in an environment that is carefully controlled to avoid contamination. These cleanrooms—so named because they are designed to be free of contaminants like dust and other particles—are often compared to surgical operating rooms due to their strict hygiene standards. In fact, many cleanrooms have higher standards for cleanliness than most hospital operating rooms. In a cleanroom, even a single speck of dust can ruin an entire microchip.

These cleanrooms are vast, often spanning eight football fields in size, and are filled with rows upon rows of sophisticated machines that perform various tasks in the chip-making process. The air is filtered through specialized systems that remove microscopic particles, ensuring that the wafers remain pristine and uncontaminated. The people who work in these cleanrooms must wear specialized clothing, including full-body suits, gloves, and face masks, to ensure that no impurities are introduced to the process.

The cleanroom environment is essential because the processes used to create microchips involve manipulating materials at an atomic scale. Each step, from the deposition of thin layers of metal to the etching of intricate circuits, requires an environment that is as free from contamination as possible. Any dust or impurity can disrupt the process, causing defects in the microchip that can render it useless.

The scale and complexity of the cleanroom operation are staggering. For example, a single chip can go through hundreds of steps, including photolithography, etching, and layering, all of which must be performed with pinpoint accuracy. A microchip might require the work of dozens of machines and thousands of precise actions before it is ready for testing and packaging.

The cleanroom is the nerve center of microchip fabrication, where raw materials are turned into the tiny yet powerful chips that run our world. In this controlled environment, scientists and engineers work tirelessly to create the next generation of technology, pushing the boundaries of what's possible with every wafer they produce.

The Cost of Innovation

The process of turning raw silicon into a finished microchip is not just highly complex but also incredibly costly. The machinery required to manufacture microchips is state-of-the-art, often costing millions of dollars per unit. These machines perform delicate operations, such as etching microscopic patterns onto the silicon wafer, and they must be maintained with the utmost care to ensure their precision. The investment in equipment is just one part of the equation; the cleanroom facilities themselves also require significant investment in terms of infrastructure, maintenance, and staffing.

Despite the immense costs involved in the microchip manufacturing process, the return on investment can be astronomical. A single silicon wafer may cost only a few hundred dollars at the outset, but once it is populated with thousands or even billions of transistors, it can be worth up to $100,000. The transformation of a simple piece of silicon into a fully functioning microchip capable of powering a range of devices is a staggering achievement of both engineering and economic value.

The high cost of microchip production is a key reason why only a select number of companies are capable of manufacturing these devices. Microchip production is an industry where scale and investment matter. The companies that dominate the market are those that have the resources to invest in the advanced technology, facilities, and expertise required to make these chips. Despite the high upfront costs, microchips have revolutionized industries across the globe, enabling innovations in fields like artificial intelligence, telecommunications, and healthcare.

In the world of microchips, cost is a reflection of both the sophistication of the technology and the potential rewards. It's a costly endeavor to create these technological marvels, but the impact they have on our lives is worth every penny.

With this first chapter, you now have an understanding of how silicon, a substance found in sand, is transformed into the sophisticated microchips that are at the heart of modern technology. It is a journey of incredible precision, immense cost, and unparalleled innovation. From the cleanroom environment to the staggering financial investments required, each step in the process highlights the incredible engineering feats that make modern electronics possible. The journey of turning sand into silicon is not just a scientific marvel but a symbol of human ingenuity—turning something as simple as sand into a cornerstone of the digital revolution.

Chapter 2

The Anatomy of a Microchip

Microchips, also known as integrated circuits (ICs), are the unseen powerhouses inside almost every electronic device. They are the tiny but mighty components responsible for executing the instructions that make our technology function. From the smartphones we carry to the servers that run the internet, microchips are at the heart of it all, working silently yet tirelessly to enable the digital world we live in.

In this chapter, we will explore the intricate anatomy of a microchip, breaking down its components, explaining how billions of transistors are packed into such a small space, and unveiling the layers of complexity that enable them to function. You'll gain insight into how the raw materials we discussed in the previous chapter are transformed into the powerful microchips that are changing the world.

What Is a Microchip?

A microchip, in its simplest form, is a small piece of silicon on which a series of electrical circuits are etched. These circuits are made up of transistors, capacitors, and resistors—each contributing a specific function within the chip's design. The primary job of a microchip is to process and transmit electrical signals, which is what allows electronic devices to perform tasks, store data, and communicate with other devices.

At the most basic level, a microchip functions much like the brain of a machine. It is responsible for interpreting and executing instructions, much like how a person reads and follows a set of directions. Microchips are designed to carry out logical functions, like adding numbers, storing and retrieving information, or processing complex algorithms, at incredible speeds. Whether in a tiny device or a massive supercomputer, microchips perform the same function—processing data and enabling the device to operate.

The components of a microchip can be broken down into three major categories:

1. Transistors – These are the most fundamental building blocks of a microchip. A transistor can be thought of as a tiny switch that can turn electrical signals on or off. By controlling the flow of electricity through the chip, transistors enable the chip to process information.

2. Capacitors – These store electrical charge, enabling the chip to perform tasks like holding data temporarily or smoothing out fluctuations in power supply.

3. Resistors – Resistors control the flow of electricity within the chip, ensuring that the signals are at the correct levels for the various circuits to function properly.

Together, these components create the integrated circuit that forms the heart of the microchip. The complexity and function of these components may seem simple at first glance, but when combined and engineered in intricate patterns, they give rise to the powerhouse that is the microchip.

Billions of Transistors, Nanometers in Size

The most striking feature of modern microchips is the sheer number of transistors packed into an incredibly tiny space. The number of transistors on a chip has grown exponentially over the years, following what is known as Moore's Law, which states that the number of transistors on a microchip doubles approximately every two years. Today, it's common to see chips with billions of transistors, all working together in perfect harmony to execute the vast array of tasks required by modern devices.

To give you a sense of scale, consider the example of a modern central processing unit (CPU), which can have up to 26 billion transistors packed into a single chip. Each of these transistors is incredibly small—often just a few nanometers (nm) in size. A nanometer is one-billionth of a meter, which is so small that it is difficult to visualize.

For reference, the width of a human hair is around 80,000 nanometers. A single transistor, depending on its technology, might be as small as 36 x 6 x 52 nm, meaning you could fit millions of transistors across the tip of a human hair.

This remarkable density of transistors has been made possible through advances in manufacturing technology. As the process of etching these transistors onto silicon wafers has become more refined, engineers have been able to shrink the transistors to smaller and smaller sizes, allowing for more to fit in the same space. The result is that microchips are now more powerful and efficient than ever before, enabling innovations in everything from artificial intelligence to quantum computing.

To put it in perspective, imagine trying to fit 26 billion tiny switches—each no bigger than a speck of dust—onto a surface the size of a fingernail. That is the incredible engineering challenge faced by microchip manufacturers today. Yet, despite this challenge, the technology has evolved to not only make this possible but to do so with unprecedented efficiency and precision.

The Dimensions: Understanding 36x6x52 Nanometer Transistors

Now that you have a sense of how many transistors can be packed into a microchip, let's take a closer look at the dimensions of these tiny components. A modern transistor, like those in today's CPUs, may measure just 36 nanometers in width, 6 nanometers in height, and 52 nanometers in length. These dimensions might sound minuscule, but they are indicative of the cutting-edge advancements in semiconductor technology.

To put this into context, the ability to fabricate transistors at such small sizes has only been made possible through advances in photolithography, a process that uses light to etch patterns onto the silicon wafer. By using ultraviolet light with extremely short wavelengths, manufacturers are able to carve out transistors with incredible precision, even at the nanometer scale.

These tiny transistors serve as the switches that control the flow of electricity through the chip. When an electrical signal is applied to a transistor, it either allows the current to flow (like a switch in the "on" position) or stops it (like a switch in the "off" position). The combination of billions of these on/off switches working in tandem allows a microchip to perform complex calculations, run algorithms, and handle everything from simple tasks to the most demanding operations.

As transistors continue to shrink in size, the number of transistors that can fit on a chip increases exponentially. This allows for more powerful chips with faster processing speeds and more advanced capabilities. However, shrinking the size of transistors also comes with its own set of challenges, such as heat dissipation and electrical interference. As engineers continue to push the limits of what is possible, the race to create smaller and more powerful transistors has led to new breakthroughs in materials, manufacturing processes, and chip architecture.

Layers and Interconnects

One of the most complex aspects of modern microchips is the intricate network of layers and interconnects that form the architecture of the chip. In addition to the transistors, capacitors, and resistors, microchips contain numerous layers of materials that are built on top of one another to create the final product. These layers serve a variety of functions, from providing electrical pathways to insulating different sections of the chip to preventing heat buildup.

Think of a microchip as an elaborate 80-layer cake—each layer contributes to the chip's ability to perform its functions. The base layer is the silicon wafer, and above it, there are layers of metal interconnects, insulating materials, and semiconductor materials, each layer playing a critical role in the chip's performance. These interconnects are the tiny electrical pathways that connect the transistors to one another, allowing the microchip to process information at lightning speed.

As the layers of a microchip are built up, each one is carefully aligned and etched with precision to ensure that the chip functions as intended. The metal interconnects that link these layers together are typically made from materials like copper or aluminum, which are good conductors of electricity. These interconnects are crucial for allowing electrical signals to travel between transistors and other components on the chip, enabling communication between different parts of the microchip.

One of the most challenging aspects of designing and manufacturing microchips is ensuring that the layers and interconnects are perfectly aligned. Any misalignment can cause electrical shorts or failures within the chip. As transistors get smaller and more layers are added, the challenge of maintaining alignment and ensuring the integrity of the interconnects becomes more difficult.

Despite these challenges, the continued miniaturization of microchips has enabled advancements in electronics that were once thought to be impossible. Today, microchips are more powerful, more efficient, and smaller than ever, with billions of transistors working together in a tightly integrated, multi-layered design.

Chapter 3

The Science Behind Microchip Manufacturing

The manufacturing process of microchips is a fascinating combination of engineering precision and cutting-edge science. Each step involves a blend of intricate technology, meticulous planning, and incredible attention to detail. From the preparation of raw silicon wafers to the creation of complex circuitry, the journey of crafting a microchip highlights the marvels of human ingenuity.

In this chapter, we will break down the five key steps in the microchip manufacturing process, delving into the intricate science behind each stage and showcasing the meticulous craftsmanship that brings these technological wonders to life.

Step 1: Preparing the Silicon Wafers

The foundation of every microchip begins with silicon wafers, which are derived from sand. Silicon is chosen due to its unique properties as a semiconductor, allowing it to conduct electricity under specific conditions. However, turning raw silicon into the perfect wafers required for microchips is no small feat.

The process begins with raw silicon extracted from quartz sand. This silicon is melted at extremely high temperatures—over 1,400°C—before being cooled and formed into large cylindrical ingots. These ingots are then sliced into thin wafers using precision saws, ensuring a consistent thickness. Each wafer is only a few millimeters thick, yet must maintain a flawless surface to ensure optimal performance during the later stages of manufacturing.

Once sliced, the wafers undergo an intense polishing process to achieve a mirror-like finish. Even the tiniest imperfection on the wafer surface can compromise the performance of the final microchip. To ensure perfection, the wafers are polished using specialized equipment and chemical solutions, removing any microscopic flaws and ensuring an ultra-smooth, uniform surface. This meticulous polishing phase not only enhances the wafer's appearance but also prepares it for the intricate steps that follow.

After polishing, the wafers are thoroughly cleaned to remove any lingering contaminants or debris. A clean surface is crucial since even microscopic particles can disrupt the photolithography process later in manufacturing. The cleaning process involves submerging the wafers in a series of chemical baths, each designed to target specific types of impurities, leaving behind nothing but pure silicon.

Finally, the prepared wafers are inspected under advanced metrology tools to ensure they meet the rigorous standards required for microchip production. These inspections involve scanning the wafers for any physical or chemical imperfections, such as scratches, irregularities, or contamination. High-resolution imaging systems and lasers are used to detect even the tiniest defects that could compromise the performance of the microchips.

The quality assurance process doesn't stop there. Wafers that pass the initial inspections undergo additional tests to verify their uniformity in thickness and flatness. These characteristics are critical because inconsistencies, even at a microscopic level, can disrupt the subsequent manufacturing steps. Once a batch of wafers meets these stringent requirements, they are carefully packaged and transported to the next stage of the manufacturing process.

This meticulous preparation process lays the foundation for all the advanced steps that follow. Without perfectly crafted wafers, the delicate and complex science of microchip manufacturing would not be possible. Each wafer is a blank canvas, ready to be transformed into a marvel of modern technology that powers everything from smartphones to space exploration.

Step 2: Creating Mask Layers

After the silicon wafers are prepared to perfection, the next phase in microchip manufacturing begins: creating the intricate patterns that will define the chip's functionality. This step is driven by photolithography, a groundbreaking process that uses light to transfer microscopic patterns onto the wafer's surface.

At its core, photolithography is like creating a stencil, but at an unimaginably small scale. It begins with the application of a thin, light-sensitive material called photoresist onto the wafer. The wafer is coated evenly to ensure precision, and this layer serves as the canvas for the chip's intricate patterns. Once the photoresist is in place, the wafer is aligned under a photomask—a template that contains the design of the microchip's circuitry.

The photomask acts like a blueprint, containing the shapes and patterns that will form the chip's transistors and connections. Light is then projected through the photomask and onto the wafer, chemically altering the photoresist wherever the light touches. This step is carried out with extreme precision, using ultraviolet (UV) light or even more advanced techniques like extreme ultraviolet (EUV) lithography for cutting-edge chips.

The regions of the photoresist exposed to light are either hardened or softened, depending on the type of photoresist used. The wafer is then treated with a chemical solution to wash away the unwanted parts of the photoresist, leaving behind the intricate patterns etched onto the wafer's surface. These patterns serve as guides for the subsequent processes, ensuring that every layer of the chip is aligned and functional.

This photolithography process is repeated multiple times to build the various layers of the microchip, each adding a new level of complexity to the design. Each iteration precisely aligns the new patterns with the existing ones, forming a three-dimensional structure on the wafer. This is crucial because even a tiny misalignment—measured in nanometers—can render the chip unusable.

To ensure this precision, manufacturers use advanced alignment systems and scanners capable of positioning the photomask with sub-nanometer accuracy. These systems are guided by sophisticated software and algorithms that monitor and adjust the process in real-time, ensuring the patterns are replicated flawlessly.

As the photolithography process progresses, the patterns become increasingly intricate. For cutting-edge chips, these patterns involve transistors and connections that are mere fractions of the width of a human hair. Extreme ultraviolet (EUV) lithography, the latest advancement in this field, uses light with a wavelength of just 13.5 nanometers to achieve these incredibly small dimensions. This allows manufacturers to pack billions of transistors onto a single microchip, enabling unprecedented computing power.

Once the patterns are complete for each layer, the wafers undergo a "baking" process to harden the remaining photoresist, ensuring it can withstand the subsequent manufacturing steps. The photolithography stage, though incredibly demanding, sets the stage for the complex electrical pathways and connections that will ultimately power devices ranging from smartphones to supercomputers.

By the time the mask layers are fully established, the silicon wafer is no longer just a blank slate. It now contains the precise roadmap for building a functioning microchip, ready for the intricate steps of transistor construction and interconnect formation that follow.

Step 3: Building the Transistors

With the mask layers in place, the next step in microchip manufacturing is constructing the transistors—the fundamental building blocks of a microchip. These microscopic components act as the switches that control the flow of electricity, enabling the chip to perform calculations, store data, and execute commands. Transistor fabrication is a highly intricate process that involves depositing, etching, and refining various materials to create these essential structures.

Deposition of Insulating and Conductive Materials

The process begins with the deposition of ultra-thin layers of materials onto the wafer's surface. These layers form the foundation for the transistor's gate, source, and drain—the three main components of a transistor. The materials used vary depending on the specific chip design but typically include insulating materials like silicon dioxide and conductive materials like polysilicon or metals such as copper and tungsten.

Deposition techniques include chemical vapor deposition (CVD) and physical vapor deposition (PVD), both of which allow for the precise application of materials at the nanometer scale. The goal is to ensure that each layer is uniform, defect-free, and perfectly aligned with the patterns created during the photolithography stage. Even the slightest inconsistency in the thickness or composition of these layers can lead to defective transistors and compromised chip performance.

Etching: Shaping the Transistor Structures

Once the materials are deposited, the next step is etching, a process that removes excess material to create the desired shapes and structures. Etching can be performed using either a chemical solution (wet etching) or plasma (dry etching), depending on the specific requirements of the design. Plasma etching, in particular, is widely used for its precision and ability to create vertical, high-aspect-ratio features.

During this stage, the intricate patterns from the mask layers guide the etching process, ensuring that only the intended areas are removed. The result is the formation of tiny trenches and features that define the transistor's geometry. These structures are measured in nanometers, with some advanced designs reaching dimensions as small as 3 nanometers—a scale so tiny that thousands of transistors could fit across the width of a single human hair.

Chemical Mechanical Planarization (CMP): Achieving a Smooth Surface

After the etching process, the wafer's surface may have uneven topography due to the creation of trenches and raised areas. To address this, the wafer undergoes chemical mechanical planarization (CMP), a critical step that smooths and flattens the surface. CMP involves polishing the wafer with a specialized slurry containing abrasive particles and chemicals that selectively remove material.

This step ensures that the wafer is perfectly flat, allowing subsequent layers to be added with precision. A smooth surface is essential for maintaining alignment between layers and ensuring the integrity of the transistor structures. Without CMP, the manufacturing process would quickly become unreliable, leading to defects and reduced yields.

Finalizing the Transistors

With the structures in place, additional materials are deposited and etched to form the final components of the transistors. For example, metal contacts are added to connect the gate, source, and drain to the rest of the circuitry. These contacts enable the flow of electrons, allowing the transistor to function as an on/off switch.

At this stage, advanced doping techniques are also used to modify the electrical properties of the silicon. By introducing impurities into specific regions of the transistor, manufacturers can control the flow of electrons and optimize the performance of the chip. These processes are carried out with nanometer-level precision to ensure that each transistor operates as intended.

.

Step 4: Adding Interconnect Layers

Once the billions of transistors have been meticulously crafted on the silicon wafer, the next critical step in microchip manufacturing involves connecting these tiny components to create functional circuits. This stage is known as the addition of interconnect layers, which serve as the wiring system that enables communication between transistors. The interconnect layers are essential for linking the chip's internal components and ensuring they work seamlessly to perform complex operations.

A Multilayered Wiring Network

The interconnect layers in a microchip are composed of incredibly thin metal wires arranged in a three-dimensional network. These wires connect the transistors to one another, as well as to the external pins or pads that interface with the outside world. To accommodate the billions of transistors on a modern microchip, the wiring must be laid out across multiple layers. Some of the most advanced chips feature over 100 interconnect layers, each carefully aligned with the others.

This multilayered structure is necessary to manage the sheer complexity of modern circuits. The layers are stacked vertically, with vias (tiny vertical connections) linking the wires between different levels. The result is a dense, intricate network that resembles a miniature skyscraper, with each layer contributing to the overall functionality of the chip.

Materials: Copper and Beyond

The choice of materials for the interconnect layers is critical to the chip's performance. Copper is the primary material used for these wires due to its excellent electrical conductivity, which minimizes resistance and power loss. Before copper became the standard, aluminum was widely used, but its higher resistance limited its efficiency in densely packed circuits. The adoption of copper revolutionized microchip performance, enabling faster, more efficient chips capable of handling the demanding applications of modern technology. In some advanced designs, even more exotic materials, such as cobalt or graphene, are being explored to further reduce resistance and improve durability.

To prevent copper from diffusing into the surrounding layers and degrading performance, a thin barrier layer is applied before the copper is deposited. This barrier, often made of materials like tantalum or titanium nitride, acts as a protective shield, ensuring the longevity and reliability of the interconnect system.

The Deposition Process: Building the Interconnect Layers

The process of creating the interconnect layers begins with the deposition of an insulating material, such as silicon dioxide or a low-k dielectric, over the wafer. This layer serves as the foundation for the metal wiring and helps to electrically isolate the various layers from one another.

Next, photolithography is used once again to define the patterns for the metal interconnects. Using advanced masks, ultraviolet light, and photoresist, the design of the wiring system is imprinted onto the wafer. Once the patterns are etched into the insulating layer, the metal deposition process begins.

Electroplating is a common technique for depositing copper into the etched trenches and vias. During electroplating, the wafer is submerged in a copper-rich solution, and an electric current is applied to encourage the copper ions to bond with the exposed areas of the wafer. This results in a uniform and thorough filling of the patterns, ensuring that the interconnects are robust and reliable.

Planarization for Perfection

After the copper is deposited, the wafer's surface is often uneven due to excess metal and the layering process. Chemical mechanical planarization (CMP) is used to smooth the surface and remove the excess copper, leaving behind only the desired interconnect patterns. This step is crucial for maintaining the precise alignment required for the layers to function correctly.

The process of patterning, depositing, and planarizing is repeated multiple times to build up the full stack of interconnect layers. As each layer is added, the chip becomes increasingly complex, with millions of connections forming the intricate circuits that define its functionality.

Addressing Signal Integrity Challenges

As the density of transistors and interconnects increases, so do the challenges related to signal integrity. Crosstalk, resistance, and capacitance between the wires can cause signal degradation, leading to slower performance or errors. To combat these issues, engineers use advanced techniques such as shielding, optimized routing, and the use of low-dielectric-constant materials to reduce interference.

Additionally, modern chips often incorporate error-correcting mechanisms and redundancy to ensure reliability. These features help to mitigate the risks posed by defects or signal disruptions, ensuring that the chip operates as intended even in challenging conditions.

Step 5: Inspection and Testing

The final step in microchip manufacturing, inspection and testing, is perhaps the most critical. It ensures that the delicate and intricate process of creating billions of transistors, layers, and interconnects results in a functional, reliable microchip. This phase uses cutting-edge tools and techniques to identify and address any flaws, guaranteeing that the chip performs as intended before it reaches the hands of consumers or industries.

The Need for Perfection

Microchips operate at a scale where even the smallest defect—a particle of dust, a microscopic crack, or an improperly etched transistor—can disrupt functionality. Given that modern chips contain billions of components working in harmony, the margin for error is virtually nonexistent. Additionally, as chips power critical technologies in healthcare, aerospace, and computing, reliability and precision are paramount.

Inspection and testing processes are designed to catch issues at every level, from the initial wafer to the finished microchip. This ensures that only the highest-quality products make it to market, while defective chips are identified and discarded or reworked early in the process.

Advanced Tools for Wafer Inspection

The first round of inspection begins with the wafer itself, even before the individual chips are separated. Specialized metrology tools are used to scan the wafer for physical and chemical imperfections. These tools include:

Scanning Electron Microscopes (SEM): SEMs provide incredibly detailed images of the wafer's surface at a nanometer scale, allowing engineers to detect minusc Advanced Tools for Wafer Inspection (continued)

Optical Inspection Systems: These high-speed cameras and lasers use advanced imaging techniques to scan the wafer's surface for visible defects, such as scratches, contamination, and even tiny irregularities in the layers. These systems provide rapid, precise feedback, allowing engineers to quickly assess the wafer's integrity.

Atomic Force Microscopes (AFM): AFMs are used to measure surface roughness at an atomic scale. This tool helps ensure that the wafer's surface is perfectly smooth, as even the smallest variations in surface texture could lead to issues during subsequent processing stages. By scanning the wafer at an incredibly fine resolution, AFMs can detect surface imperfections that might not be visible under optical inspection, ensuring a perfectly smooth foundation for the next steps in chip manufacturing.

X-ray Inspection Tools: X-ray systems are used to examine the internal structure of the wafer, particularly the interconnect layers and any buried components. These tools generate detailed images that reveal potential issues such as voids, misalignments, or other hidden defects within the chip's layered structure. Non-invasive, X-ray inspection plays a vital role in detecting internal flaws that could affect performance but are difficult to catch using traditional methods.

These advanced tools work together to provide a comprehensive assessment of the wafer's quality. They ensure that defects are detected and addressed before the wafer is cut into individual microchips, minimizing the risk of faulty chips reaching the final product stage. Every inspection step is a critical part of ensuring the microchip meets the exacting standards required for modern technology.

Chapter 4

Precision Engineering in the Fabrication Plant

Microchip manufacturing represents the pinnacle of precision engineering, where every detail matters. The fabrication plant, or "fab," is the beating heart of this process, housing advanced machinery and technologies that turn silicon wafers into microchips. Each of the 940 meticulous steps in the process is executed with near-perfect accuracy to ensure the final product meets stringent standards. This chapter explores the indispensable role of machines, the importance of automation, and the strategies for avoiding defects in this complex environment.

The Role of Machines

Microchip fabrication is a highly intricate process requiring specialized tools that execute specific functions with unparalleled precision. These machines can be grouped into four essential categories: cleaning, etching, depositing, and inspecting.

Cleaning Machines

Before any processing begins, wafers must be spotless. Cleaning tools use a combination of chemical baths, deionized water, and ultrasonic vibrations to remove any residual particles, organic matter, or oxidation layers. The cleaning phase is so critical that even a particle smaller than a human hair can compromise the wafer's integrity.

The cleanroom environment in which these tools operate further ensures that contaminants are kept to an absolute minimum. Air is filtered multiple times per minute, and technicians wear specialized suits to prevent any dust or skin particles from interfering with the wafers.

Etching Machines

Etching tools create the microscopic patterns that define a chip's circuitry. Using either wet chemical solutions or plasma-based dry etching, these machines remove precise portions of material from the wafer's surface.

Dry etching, in particular, is favored for its ability to achieve nanoscale precision. It involves bombarding the wafer's surface with ionized gases that chemically react to carve out the desired structures. The etching process ensures that each transistor and circuit is perfectly formed, down to the atomic level.

Deposition Machines

To build up the layers of a microchip, deposition machines add ultra-thin films of material—ranging from metals like copper to insulators like silicon dioxide. Techniques such as chemical vapor deposition (CVD) and physical vapor deposition (PVD) are employed to ensure uniform coverage across the wafer.

Atomic layer deposition (ALD), a more advanced technique, allows for even greater precision, depositing layers only a few atoms thick. These deposited films form the foundation of transistors, interconnects, and other essential chip components.

Inspection Machines

Inspection tools are responsible for ensuring quality at every step. These machines use advanced imaging technologies, such as scanning electron microscopes (SEM), optical inspection systems, and atomic force microscopes (AFM), to detect defects as small as a few nanometers.

For instance, SEMs provide detailed images of the wafer's surface, allowing engineers to verify the accuracy of etched patterns. Optical systems, on the other hand, scan for larger defects like scratches or contamination. Together, these tools form the backbone of quality control in the fab.

How Automation Enhances Precision

One of the defining features of modern fabs is the integration of automation, which ensures consistency and minimizes human error. Automated systems handle tasks ranging from wafer transportation to data analysis, streamlining the entire manufacturing process.

Wafer Handling

In traditional manufacturing, human handling introduces the risk of contamination. Automated robots eliminate this risk by moving wafers between tools in sealed, contamination-free pods. These robots operate with extreme precision, ensuring that wafers are always positioned correctly for each process step.

Process Control

Automation also extends to process monitoring. Sensors embedded in machines continuously track critical variables like temperature, pressure, and chemical composition. Advanced software analyzes this data in real-time, allowing engineers to detect and address anomalies before they escalate.

This level of precision enables fabs to produce thousands of microchips with near-perfect consistency, meeting the high demands of industries like computing, telecommunications, and healthcare.

Avoiding Defects

In a process as complex as microchip fabrication, even a single defect can have catastrophic consequences. The stakes are particularly high given the 940-step process required to create a functional chip.

The Risks of Mistakes

Microchips operate at a scale where even minor defects—such as a misaligned layer or an incomplete etch—can render an entire wafer unusable. These errors not only lead to wasted materials but also increase production costs and delay delivery times.

Defects are especially problematic in industries like aerospace or medical devices, where chip failures could have life-threatening consequences. As a result, fabs prioritize quality control at every stage of manufacturing.

Continuous Monitoring for Quality

To prevent defects, fabs employ continuous monitoring systems that provide real-time feedback on every aspect of the manufacturing process. For example, tools like in-line metrology systems measure wafer thickness and uniformity after each step, ensuring that no deviations occur.

Additionally, advanced analytics platforms use machine learning algorithms to predict potential issues before they arise. By analyzing historical data, these systems can identify patterns and suggest corrective actions, further enhancing yield rates.

Proactive Defect Management

When defects are detected, fabs take immediate action to address the root cause. This may involve recalibrating a machine, adjusting process parameters, or reworking affected wafers. Engineers conduct thorough investigations to ensure that similar issues do not occur in the future.

Chapter 6

The Challenges of Microchip Manufacturing

The production of microchips is one of the most complex and demanding processes in modern industry. As technology evolves, manufacturers face increasing challenges to meet the demand for smaller, faster, and more efficient chips. This chapter explores the key hurdles in microchip manufacturing, including the physics of scaling down to nanometers and the financial and environmental costs of production.

Scaling Down to Nanometers

The relentless pursuit of smaller and more powerful microchips has driven the industry to push the boundaries of physics. Modern chips operate at nanometer scales, where the size of a single transistor is measured in billionths of a meter. This continuous shrinking of transistors has fueled exponential growth in computational power, as predicted by Moore's Law. However, as dimensions approach atomic scales, manufacturers face unprecedented technical challenges.

The Physics of Working at Atomic Scales

At nanometer scales, the behavior of materials is governed by quantum mechanics rather than classical physics. Electrons, for example, can "tunnel" through barriers that would be insurmountable at larger scales. This quantum tunneling effect leads to leakage currents, which waste energy and generate heat, reducing chip efficiency.

In addition, as transistors shrink, it becomes increasingly difficult to maintain uniformity in their fabrication. Even minor variations in material properties or processing conditions can lead to significant performance inconsistencies.

Limitations and Breakthroughs in Transistor Miniaturization

The shrinking of transistors has also reached fundamental material limits. For example, silicon—the backbone of microchip technology—loses its insulating properties when scaled below a certain thickness. To overcome this, researchers have turned to advanced materials like silicon-germanium alloys and even two-dimensional materials like graphene.

Another breakthrough is the adoption of three-dimensional transistor architectures, such as FinFETs (Fin Field-Effect Transistors) and GAAFETs (Gate-All-Around FETs). These designs maximize control over electrical currents while minimizing leakage, enabling further scaling. However, implementing these technologies requires significant investments in new manufacturing tools and processes, adding complexity and cost to chip production.

Cost and Resource Challenges

Microchip manufacturing is an expensive and resource-intensive endeavor, with each new generation of chips pushing the limits of what is financially and environmentally sustainable. The race to innovate must be balanced against the economic and ecological impact of production.

The Financial Costs of Microchip Production

Building and operating a state-of-the-art fabrication plant requires billions of dollars in investment. For example, advanced EUV lithography machines used to etch the finest features onto wafers can cost over $150 million each. The complexity of the process also drives up costs, with each new node requiring additional steps and stricter quality controls.

R&D expenses are another significant burden. As manufacturers push the boundaries of physics, they must invest heavily in developing new materials, architectures, and manufacturing techniques. This financial strain is compounded by fierce competition in the semiconductor industry, where the first to market with cutting-edge chips often dominates.

The Environmental Costs of Microchip Manufacturing

The environmental impact of microchip production is another pressing concern. Fabs consume enormous amounts of energy, with some requiring as much electricity as a small city. Additionally, the production process involves the use of hazardous chemicals, including solvents, acids, and gases, which must be carefully managed to prevent environmental contamination.

Water usage is another critical issue. Manufacturing a single silicon wafer can consume thousands of gallons of ultra-pure water, which must be treated and recycled to minimize waste. As global demand for chips continues to grow, the industry faces mounting pressure to adopt more sustainable practices.

Balancing Innovation with Sustainability

To address these challenges, chipmakers are investing in greener technologies and practices. For instance, fabs are adopting energy-efficient equipment, renewable energy sources, and advanced waste treatment systems. Circular manufacturing models, where materials are recycled and reused, are also gaining traction.

In addition, industry collaborations aim to develop global standards for sustainability in semiconductor manufacturing. By sharing best practices and pooling resources, chipmakers can reduce their environmental footprint while maintaining the pace of innovation.

Chapter 7

Testing, Packaging, and Delivery

After the intricate processes of manufacturing and assembling billions of transistors, microchip production enters its final stages. This phase includes rigorous testing to ensure quality, precise cutting and packaging to protect the chips, and efficient logistics to deliver them to consumers. These steps are crucial in transforming the raw output of the fabrication plant into ready-to-use components that power modern devices.

Testing the Chips

Rigorous Tests to Ensure Perfection

Microchips must undergo a battery of rigorous tests to ensure they meet the highest standards of quality and reliability. Testing begins while the chips are still part of the silicon wafer. Specialized equipment examines electrical signals to verify that each transistor, interconnect, and layer performs as expected.

Post-wafer testing, known as wafer probing, uses precision probes to check the functionality of individual chips. Engineers look for defects such as short circuits, weak signals, or electrical leakage. These tests are crucial because even a single faulty transistor can compromise the chip's performance.

Once the chips are cut from the wafer, further tests are conducted. These include:

Functional Testing: Verifying that the chip performs its intended operations correctly.

Thermal Testing: Ensuring the chip can operate within specified temperature ranges.

Stress Testing: Subjecting the chip to extreme conditions to identify potential points of failure.

Categorization Based on Performance and Functionality

Chips that pass testing are categorized based on their performance and functionality. Variations in silicon quality and manufacturing precision can lead to slight differences in speed and efficiency among chips produced from the same wafer. This process, known as binning, allows manufacturers to group chips into different performance tiers.

For instance, high-performance chips may be sold as premium products, while slightly lower-performing chips are marketed for budget-friendly applications. This approach ensures optimal utilization of every chip, minimizing waste and maximizing profitability.

Cutting and Packaging

How Individual Chips Are Cut from Wafers

After testing, the wafer undergoes a process called dicing, where individual chips are separated. Dicing is performed using precision tools like diamond-tipped saws or laser cutters, which can slice through the wafer with incredible accuracy. The goal is to minimize damage to the delicate circuitry while ensuring clean cuts.

Once separated, each chip is inspected for any damage caused during the dicing process. Damaged chips are discarded, while intact ones move on to the next stage: packaging.

Assembling and Packaging for End Use

Packaging is a critical step that protects the chip and prepares it for integration into devices. The process begins by placing each chip onto a substrate, which serves as a base for electrical connections. The chip is then encapsulated in a protective material, such as epoxy resin, to shield it from physical damage, moisture, and environmental contaminants.

Key components of the packaging process include:

Bonding Wires or Flip-Chip Connections: Establishing electrical connections between the chip and the substrate.

Heat Spreaders: Adding components to dissipate heat generated during operation.

Marking: Printing identification codes and branding on the package for traceability.

Advanced packaging techniques, such as 3D stacking, are becoming more common. These methods allow multiple chips to be integrated into a single package, improving performance and reducing space requirements.

Chapter 8

The Science Driving the Future of Microchips

Microchips, often described as the lifeblood of modern technology, have undergone remarkable transformations since their inception. These advancements are deeply rooted in scientific innovation, driven by the need to create smaller, faster, and more energy-efficient devices. The evolution of transistor technology has been pivotal in this journey, as it directly determines the computational power and efficiency of microchips. At the same time, the challenges of miniaturization, heat dissipation, and material limitations continue to push researchers and engineers to explore new horizons in semiconductor manufacturing.

The future of microchips lies in breakthroughs that will redefine their design and functionality. Emerging technologies such as quantum computing, artificial intelligence (AI), and machine learning are opening doors to a new era of computational possibilities. These innovations not only shape the capabilities of future chips but also have far-reaching implications for industries like healthcare, communication, transportation, and beyond. Understanding the science behind these advancements offers a glimpse into how microchips will drive the technologies of tomorrow.

The Evolution of Transistor Technology

Transistors, the building blocks of microchips, have come a long way since their introduction in the mid-20th century. The planar transistor, first developed in 1959, marked the beginning of the microelectronics revolution. These early transistors were relatively large compared to modern standards, but they laid the groundwork for the rapid miniaturization that followed. Over the decades, engineers consistently pushed the boundaries of Moore's

Law, doubling the number of transistors on a chip approximately every two years. This relentless progress transformed bulky computers into sleek, powerful devices that fit in the palm of your hand.

One of the most significant milestones in transistor technology was the shift from planar transistors to FinFETs (fin field-effect transistors). Introduced in the early 2000s, FinFET technology represented a major leap in performance and efficiency. Unlike planar transistors, which lie flat on the chip's surface, FinFETs feature a three-dimensional "fin" structure that allows for better control of electrical current. This innovation significantly reduced power leakage and enabled chips to operate at lower voltages, making them ideal for modern applications such as smartphones, wearables, and data centers.

As the industry approaches the physical limits of silicon-based transistors, researchers are exploring new materials and designs to sustain progress. Gate-all-around (GAA) transistors, for instance, are poised to replace FinFETs in the near future. GAA technology further enhances current control by surrounding the channel with gates on all sides, enabling even greater miniaturization and efficiency. This shift is critical as manufacturers strive to produce chips with features measured in nanometers, a scale where quantum effects start to influence performance.

Beyond traditional transistor technology, the push toward quantum computing represents a paradigm shift in computational science. Unlike classical computers, which process information in binary (1s and 0s), quantum computers use qubits that can exist in multiple states simultaneously. This allows quantum systems to perform complex calculations at unprecedented speeds, making them ideal for tasks like cryptography, drug discovery, and climate modeling. However, quantum computing is still in its infancy, and significant challenges remain in scaling and stabilizing these systems for practical use.

Another promising development is the emergence of 3D chip architectures. Traditional chips are designed in a flat, two-dimensional layout, but stacking multiple layers of transistors vertically allows for greater performance density and energy efficiency. This approach not only reduces the physical footprint of microchips but also enables faster data transfer between layers, making them ideal for high-performance applications like AI and machine learning.

Emerging Challenges

As microchips become increasingly powerful, they also face significant challenges that threaten to slow their progress. One of the most pressing issues is heat dissipation. As transistors shrink and operate at higher speeds, they generate more heat in smaller areas. This can lead to thermal management problems that compromise performance and reliability. Engineers are exploring advanced cooling solutions, such as liquid cooling and thermoelectric materials, to address these issues. Additionally, researchers are investigating the use of materials with higher thermal conductivity, such as graphene and diamond, to improve heat dissipation at the chip level.

Power consumption is another critical concern. Modern devices, from smartphones to data centers, require enormous amounts of energy to function. As the demand for computational power grows, so does the need for energy-efficient chips. Low-power design techniques, such as dynamic voltage scaling and power gating, are helping to reduce energy consumption. At the same time, alternative energy sources, such as solar-powered chips, are being explored to minimize the environmental impact of semiconductor manufacturing.

Material limitations also pose significant challenges to the future of microchips. Silicon, the primary material used in semiconductors, is approaching its physical limits in terms of size and performance. To overcome this, researchers are experimenting with new materials like gallium nitride (GaN) and molybdenum disulfide (MoS2), which offer superior electrical properties and greater scalability. These materials have the potential to replace silicon in next-generation chips, enabling further miniaturization and improved efficiency.

Another emerging challenge is the increasing complexity of chip design and manufacturing. As transistors become smaller and more intricate, the cost and time required to develop new chips have skyrocketed. Advanced tools, such as extreme ultraviolet (EUV) lithography, are essential for producing nanometer-scale features, but they come with significant financial and technical hurdles. Collaboration between academia, industry, and government is crucial to overcome these obstacles and ensure the continued advancement of microchip technology.

The Future of Semiconductor Manufacturing

The future of semiconductor manufacturing is being shaped by transformative technologies that promise to redefine the capabilities of microchips. Artificial intelligence and machine learning are playing an increasingly important role in chip design, enabling engineers to optimize layouts, predict performance, and identify potential issues with unprecedented accuracy. These tools accelerate the design process and reduce costs, making it easier to develop chips for specialized applications.

AI-driven chip design is particularly important for the development of edge computing devices, which process data locally rather than relying on centralized data centers. This approach reduces latency, improves security, and enables real-time decision-making, making it ideal for applications like autonomous vehicles, smart cities, and industrial automation. By leveraging AI in the design process, manufacturers can create chips that are tailored to the specific needs of these emerging technologies.

The Internet of Things (IoT) is another area where microchips are set to have a profound impact. IoT devices, ranging from smart home appliances to industrial sensors, rely on advanced microchips to collect and process data. As the number of IoT devices continues to grow, the demand for specialized chips that balance performance, energy efficiency, and security will only increase. Manufacturers are responding by developing chips with integrated AI capabilities, enabling IoT devices to make intelligent decisions without relying on external processing.

Autonomous systems, such as self-driving cars and drones, represent yet another frontier for microchip innovation. These systems require chips that can process vast amounts of data in real time while ensuring safety and reliability. Advances in neural network accelerators and sensor integration are driving the development of chips that can meet these demanding requirements. The impact of these technologies extends beyond transportation, with potential applications in agriculture, healthcare, and disaster response.

As the semiconductor industry looks to the future, sustainability is becoming an increasingly important consideration. The environmental impact of microchip production, including energy consumption, water usage, and waste generation, is prompting manufacturers to adopt more sustainable practices. This includes the use of renewable energy, recycling of materials, and the development of greener manufacturing processes. By prioritizing sustainability, the industry can ensure that microchips continue to drive innovation while minimizing their environmental footprint.

The science driving the future of microchips is a testament to human ingenuity and determination. As researchers and engineers overcome the challenges of miniaturization, heat dissipation, and material limitations, they are paving the way for a new era of technological progress. With advancements in AI, quantum computing, and 3D architectures, microchips will continue to play a central role in shaping the world of tomorrow.

Chapter 9

The Microchip Revolution – A Global Perspective

The microchip, a marvel of modern engineering, has become the cornerstone of technological advancement and human progress. This tiny device, often smaller than a fingernail, powers the tools, systems, and innovations that define the modern world. From the smartphones in our hands to the satellites orbiting Earth, microchips drive the functions of nearly every piece of advanced technology we rely on today. However, the importance of microchips extends beyond individual devices. They form the backbone of entire industries, shaping economies, geopolitics, and the future of human development.

The microchip revolution began with the invention of the integrated circuit in the mid-20th century, but its impact has only grown exponentially in recent decades. The rapid miniaturization and increased efficiency of these chips have enabled technological breakthroughs that were once the stuff of science fiction. As industries and governments recognize the critical role microchips play, the global dependence on these tiny devices has transformed them into strategic assets, vital for innovation and security alike.

Yet, this dependence also introduces challenges. The demand for microchips has surged to unprecedented levels, often outpacing supply, which has led to global shortages affecting industries from automotive manufacturing to consumer electronics. The competition to secure a reliable supply chain has intensified, giving rise to geopolitical rivalries and significant investments in semiconductor manufacturing capabilities. Understanding the profound effects of this revolution requires examining the dual aspects of global dependence on microchips and the geopolitical dynamics shaping their production.

Global Dependence on Microchips

Microchips have become the lifeblood of modern industries, serving as the critical components that enable technological innovation. In healthcare, microchips power sophisticated diagnostic machines, wearable health monitors, and life-saving medical devices like pacemakers. These chips enable real-time data collection and analysis, which improves patient care and supports groundbreaking medical research. Without microchips, the advancements in telemedicine and personalized healthcare that we see today would be unimaginable.

In the realm of communication, microchips have revolutionized the way people connect. They are the foundation of the telecommunications industry, enabling the creation and maintenance of global networks. Smartphones, tablets, and laptops—all equipped with advanced microchips—allow individuals to communicate across continents in seconds. Beyond personal use, microchips are at the core of cloud computing and data centers, where vast amounts of information are stored and processed. These advancements have laid the groundwork for global collaboration and knowledge sharing, redefining the boundaries of what is possible in business and everyday life.

The transportation sector is another area where microchips have become indispensable. Modern vehicles rely on complex electronic control units (ECUs) that use microchips to manage everything from engine performance to advanced safety features like lane assist and automatic braking. The rise of electric vehicles (EVs) and autonomous driving technology has further emphasized the role of microchips, as these innovations depend heavily on advanced processing power and real-time decision-making capabilities. With microchips enabling efficient energy management and navigation systems, the future of transportation is being reshaped before our eyes.

Microchips are also at the heart of industrial automation and robotics, which have transformed manufacturing processes worldwide. These chips enable precision control, reduce production costs, and increase efficiency, allowing companies to scale their operations while maintaining quality. In agriculture, microchips power smart farming tools, such as automated irrigation systems and drones used for crop monitoring, leading to increased productivity and sustainability.

Perhaps the most transformative role of microchips is in the technology that drives innovation itself—artificial intelligence (AI) and machine learning. AI relies on powerful processors to analyze data, recognize patterns, and make decisions. From virtual assistants like Siri and Alexa to complex algorithms that predict climate change or detect financial fraud, microchips enable AI systems to function seamlessly. This has far-reaching implications for society, as AI continues to revolutionize industries and improve quality of life.

However, this global dependence on microchips comes with vulnerabilities. The growing demand for semiconductors has strained the supply chain, leading to shortages that ripple across industries. For instance, during the COVID-19 pandemic, the global chip shortage disrupted the production of automobiles, consumer electronics, and even medical equipment. This highlighted the fragility of the supply chain and the importance of ensuring its resilience. As industries continue to rely on microchips for innovation, addressing these challenges becomes a priority for governments and businesses alike.

The Geopolitics of Semiconductors

As the importance of microchips has grown, so too has the competition to control their production and supply. The semiconductor industry is highly concentrated, with a few key players dominating the market. Countries with advanced semiconductor manufacturing capabilities, such as the United States, Taiwan, South Korea, and China, hold significant strategic advantages. This concentration of power has led to intense geopolitical rivalries, as nations vie for dominance in this critical sector.

Taiwan, home to the world's leading semiconductor manufacturer, Taiwan Semiconductor Manufacturing Company (TSMC), plays a pivotal role in the global supply chain. TSMC produces chips for some of the largest technology companies, including Apple, NVIDIA, and Qualcomm. This makes Taiwan a crucial player in the technology ecosystem, but it also makes the region a focal point of geopolitical tensions. The strategic importance of Taiwan's semiconductor industry has drawn international attention, with nations seeking to safeguard the supply chain from potential disruptions.

China, recognizing the importance of self-reliance in semiconductor manufacturing, has invested heavily in building its domestic capabilities. The Chinese government's Made in China 2025 initiative aims to reduce dependence on foreign chipmakers and establish China as a global leader in advanced technologies. However, achieving this goal has proven challenging, as China faces restrictions on accessing cutting-edge manufacturing equipment and technologies due to trade tensions with the United States.

The United States, for its part, has taken significant steps to strengthen its semiconductor industry. In recent years, the U.S. government has introduced policies and funding to encourage domestic chip production and research. Initiatives like the CHIPS Act aim to reduce reliance on foreign suppliers and ensure the security of the semiconductor supply chain. By fostering collaboration between the public and private sectors, the U.S. seeks to maintain its technological edge in the face of global competition.

South Korea is another major player in the semiconductor industry, with companies like Samsung and SK Hynix leading in memory chip production. South Korea's expertise in this area has made it a key contributor to the global supply chain, further solidifying its position as a technological powerhouse.

The geopolitics of semiconductors also extends to Europe, where nations are investing in strengthening their semiconductor ecosystems. The European Union has launched initiatives to increase chip production and reduce dependency on external suppliers, recognizing the strategic importance of semiconductors for economic and technological sovereignty.

Maintaining a secure supply chain for semiconductors is a pressing concern for all nations involved. Disruptions in the supply chain, whether due to natural disasters, trade disputes, or geopolitical conflicts, can have far-reaching consequences. Ensuring a stable and reliable supply of microchips requires international cooperation, investment in research and development, and diversification of manufacturing capabilities.

Conclusion

Microchips, often unseen and underappreciated, are nothing short of a modern miracle. Their journey from mere scientific curiosity to an indispensable cornerstone of daily life is a testament to human innovation and resilience. These tiny silicon wafers have grown to become the bedrock of the digital era, silently powering the devices and systems that shape our personal and professional lives. From the smartphones in our hands to the satellites orbiting Earth, microchips are everywhere, seamlessly enabling connections, automation, and advancements that define modern civilization.

It is easy to overlook the complexity and science behind these technological wonders. Few people stop to consider the intricate processes and relentless innovation that go into creating a chip. The fabrication plants, operating at atomic scales, embody the pinnacle of precision engineering, while the transistor technologies and cutting-edge designs reflect decades of tireless research and development. Behind every microchip lies the dedication of countless engineers, scientists, and visionaries who have pushed the boundaries of what's possible.

Reflecting on the journey of microchips reveals a story of progress unlike any other. Their evolution is marked by transformative leaps, from planar transistors to FinFETs, from silicon-based designs to the promise of quantum computing and AI-optimized architectures. Each breakthrough has been driven by a profound need to make technology smaller, faster, and more energy-efficient, ensuring that the world keeps pace with an ever-growing demand for computational power.

More than just technological achievements, microchips are emblematic of human creativity and perseverance. They remind us that even the smallest innovations can lead to monumental changes in how we live, work, and interact. They serve as a bridge between imagination and reality, turning once-distant dreams of artificial intelligence, smart cities, and autonomous systems into tangible advancements. By recognizing their profound impact, we can cultivate a deeper appreciation for the science and engineering behind the tools we use every day.

As we stand on the threshold of the future, the role of microchips will only grow in importance. Emerging technologies like the Internet of Things, quantum computing, and AI are set to redefine the limits of human potential. However, the journey ahead is not without challenges. Issues such as rising costs, resource constraints, and environmental impact present significant hurdles that must be addressed with urgency and innovation.

The call to action for the semiconductor industry is clear: progress must be balanced with sustainability. Manufacturers must prioritize greener production methods, reduce energy consumption, and explore alternative materials that minimize environmental harm. This is not merely a responsibility—it is an opportunity to redefine the industry's legacy and ensure its relevance in a world increasingly focused on sustainability.

At the same time, global collaboration will be essential. The geopolitics of semiconductors remind us that microchip innovation is a shared endeavor, requiring the collective efforts of nations, organizations, and individuals. By fostering partnerships and investing in education, research, and infrastructure, the global community can overcome the barriers that threaten the industry's future.

The road ahead also requires us, as individuals, to remain curious and informed. By understanding the science behind microchips, we can better appreciate the profound impact they have on our lives and support efforts to advance their development. Whether it's advocating for more investment in semiconductor research or simply acknowledging the value of technology in our daily routines, everyone has a role to play in shaping the future of microchips.